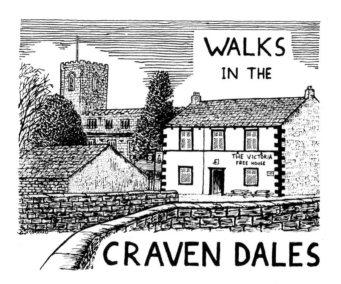

WALKS
IN THE

THE VICTORIA
FREE HOUSE

CRAVEN DALES

HILLSIDE GUIDES

LONG DISTANCE WALKS

1 • THE WESTMORLAND WAY
2 • THE FURNESS WAY
3 • THE CUMBERLAND WAY
7 • CLEVELAND WAY COMPANION
9 • THE NORTH BOWLAND TRAVERSE
(by David Johnson)
16 • DALES WAY COMPANION

CIRCULAR WALKS - YORKSHIRE DALES

4 • WALKS IN WHARFEDALE
5 • WALKS IN NIDDERDALE
6 • WALKS IN THE CRAVEN DALES
8 • WALKS IN WENSLEYDALE
10 • WALKS IN THE WESTERN DALES
11 • WALKS IN SWALEDALE

CIRCULAR WALKS - NORTH YORK MOORS

13 • WESTERN - Cleveland/Hambleton Hills
14 • SOUTHERN - Rosedale/Farndale/Bransdale
15 • NORTHERN - Eskdale and the Coast

CIRCULAR WALKS - SOUTH PENNINES

12 • WALKS IN BRONTE COUNTRY
17 • WALKS IN CALDERDALE

HILLWALKING - THE LAKE DISTRICT

18 • OVER LAKELAND MOUNTAINS
19 • OVER LAKELAND FELLS

---

80 DALES WALKS
Published by Cordee, Leicester
An omnibus edition combining Books 4, 6, 8, 10, 11

WALKS
IN THE
CRAVEN DALES

by

Paul Hannon

HILLSIDE PUBLICATIONS

HILLSIDE PUBLICATIONS
11 Nessfield Grove
Exley Head
Keighley
West Yorkshire
BD22 6NU

First published 1986
3rd impression 1990

Cover illustration: Malham Cove
Page 1: Kirkby Malham

ISBN   0 9509212 6 2

Printed in Great Britain by
Carnmor Print and Design
95/97 London Road
Preston
Lancashire
PR1 4BA

INTRODUCTION

The Aire is one of the major rivers of Yorkshire yet unlike it's neighbours which also rise high in the Dales, the Aire has but a brief existance in these tranquil pastures before heading into the heart of industrial Yorkshire. Fortunately it's time inside the National Park is a well-spent one, and along with it's numerous tributary becks provides a highly compact area to which this guide is dedicated. The title of this work may arouse some interest: Craven was the name given to an area much larger than that looked at in these pages, stretching further up into the Dales and also down to the lowlands south and west of Skipton. With 'Upper Airedale' a non-starter, the title 'Malhamdale' is usually given to that part of Airedale within the Dales, but is of little value here as it fails to include the fine walking country east of the Aire., an area often ignored or at best inexplicably included in Wharfedale. To sum up then; our area is in the heart of Craven and is certainly in the Dales: what else could it possibly be called?

Not only is this a compact area, it is a richly contrasting one. The western half needs little introduction, for the Malham district is renowned for it's stunningly impressive limestone scenery, with Malham Cove and Gordale Scar known to almost everyone. East of Malhamdale the surroundings change dramatically: here is typical millstone-grit country, with rocky outcrops, bracken-covered slopes and some splendid heather moorland. The boundary of the Craven Dales is well-defined by the watersheds with the Ribble, Skirfare and Wharfe to the west, north and east respectively, and by the extremity of the National Park boundary to the south.

Standing at this boundary is Skipton, a fascinating market town known as the 'Gateway to the Dales'. It makes an ideal base for the Craven area and is an interesting place in it's own right. It's many attractions include the Castle (a must), the Parish Church, the spacious High Street, the Craven Museum and the Leeds—Liverpool Canal. The market operates on Wednesday, Friday and Saturday, and early-closing is on Tuesday.

The 16 walks described range in length from 3½ to 10 miles, and the terrain similarly varies from green pastures to rather more strenuous moorland walking. All are circular walks, and with an average distance of just over 6 miles, they are ideally suited to half-day rambles. Each has it's own chapter consisting of 'immediate impression' diagram, detailed narrative and strip-map, and notes and illustrations of features of interest along the way.

All of the miles covered are on public rights-of-way, other than Walks 5 and 14 which cross the Barden Moor Access Area. This vast tract of moorland is part of the Duke of Devonshire's estates, and a negotiated agreement allows access to walk other than on a limited number of days when shooting takes place. (all Sundays are safe)

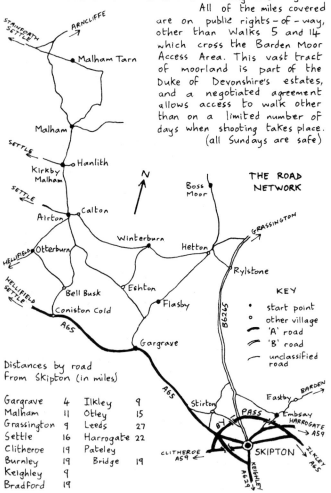

THE ROAD NETWORK

KEY

- • start point
- ○ other village
- ▬ 'A' road
- ⁓ 'B' road
- — unclassified road

Distances by road from Skipton (in miles)

Gargrave	4	Ilkley	9
Malham	11	Otley	15
Grassington	9	Leeds	27
Settle	16	Harrogate	22
Clitheroe	19	Pateley	
Burnley	19	Bridge	19
Keighley	9		
Bradford	19		

6

	Accommodation	Inn	Car Park	Bus service	Post Office	Shop	Toilets
Airton	✓	–	–	✓	✓	–	–
Bell Busk	✓	–	–	–	✓	–	–
Eastby	–	✓	–	✓	–	–	–
Embsay	✓	✓	✓	✓	✓	✓	–
Eshton	✓	–	–	✓	–	–	–
Flasby	–	–	–	–	–	–	–
Gargrave	✓	✓	✓	✓	✓	✓	✓
Hetton	✓	✓	–	✓	–	–	–
Kirkby Malham	✓	✓	–	✓	–	–	–
Malham	✓	✓	✓	✓	✓	✓	✓
Otterburn	–	–	–	–	–	–	–
Rylstone	–	–	–	✓	–	–	–
Stirton	✓	✓	–	–	–	–	–
Winterburn	–	–	–	–	–	–	–

As can readily be seen, many of the smaller villages are devoid of visitor facilities. As already noted, Skipton is an incomparable base for the area, but Malham and Gargrave both cater adequately for walkers, while retaining their village atmosphere. The only youth hostel is at Malham: outside of this area Stainforth and Linton hostels provide useful links with it. Toilets/car parks listed are in addition to the usual inn-facilities, whilst the other subjects listed are inevitably prone to alteration. There is a camp-site at Gargrave and a Mountain-Rescue Post at Malham.

ORDNANCE SURVEY MAPS

Although the strip-maps illustrating each walk are sufficient to guide one safely around, they do nothing to show the surrounding countryside. The obvious answer is an Ordnance Survey map, as follows:

1:50,000 metric scale
sheet 98: Wensleydale + Wharfedale
sheet 103: Blackburn + Burnley
sheet 104: Leeds + Bradford

1 inch to the mile
sheet 90: Wensleydale
sheet 95: Blackburn + Burnley
sheet 96: Leeds + Bradford

Interestingly, on the larger scale of 1:25,000 (2½ inches to the mile) one sheet covers the _whole_ of this guide's territory, namely 'Outdoor Leisure Map No.10 – Yorkshire Dales 'Southern Area'

PUBLIC TRANSPORT

Railway stations are located at Gargrave and Skipton, with the latter having a more regular connection with West Yorkshire and points further afield. Bus services radiate from Skipton to many of the villages, either by 'West Yorkshire' or, in Malhamdale, the locally-run 'Pennine'.

INNS AND BEER

Outside of Skipton itself (which boasts a fine range of inns) the area is sparsely-covered with licensed premises. Fortunately almost all those that exist sell traditional beer. Beyond the two larger villages of Embsay and Gargrave the inns are thinly-scattered, and free-houses are few. A rare surprise can be found on the buffet-car of Embsay's steam railway. The following brews can generally be relied upon - with a little care in Skipton. The last two are found only in Skipton town.

Taylor, Keighley   Theakston, Masham and Carlisle
Younger, Edinburgh   Bass, Tadcaster   Tetley, Leeds
Whitbread, Castle Eden and Salford   Webster, Halifax
Thwaites, Blackburn   Hartley, Ulverston

SOME USEFUL ADDRESSES

Ramblers' Association
   1/5 Wandsworth Road, London SW8 2XX
     Tel. 01 - 582 6878

Youth Hostels Association
   Trevelyan House, St. Albans, Herts. AL1 2DY
     Tel. St. Albans (0727) 55215

Yorkshire Dales National Park
   Office and Information Centre
   Colvend, Hebden Road, Grassington,
   Skipton, North Yorkshire BD23 5LB
     Tel. Grassington (0756) 752748

   Malham Information Centre
     Tel. Airton (07293) 363
   (April to October and winter weekends)

Skipton Tourist Information
   Victoria Square, Skipton
     Tel. Skipton (0756) 2809

Yorkshire and·Humberside Tourist Board
   312 Tadcaster Road, York YO2 2HF
     Tel. York (0904) 707961

Yorkshire Dales Society
   152 Main Street, Addingham, Ilkley,
   West Yorkshire LS29 0LY

West Yorkshire Road Car Company
   PO Box 24, East Parade, Harrogate,
   North Yorkshire HG1 5LS
     Tel. Harrogate (0423) 66061
   Local enquiries - Tel. Skipton (0756) 5331

Pennine Motors
   Main Street, Gargrave, Skipton, N. Yorkshire
     Tel. Skipton (0756) 749215

Bolton Abbey Estate Office (Barden Moor access area)
   Tel. Bolton Abbey (075671) 227

THE WALKS

Listed below are the 16 walks described, the walk number being the key to easy location in the guide

THE WALKS

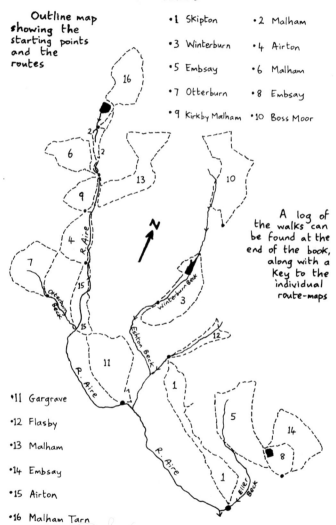

Outline map showing the starting points and the routes

A log of the walks can be found at the end of the book, along with a Key to the individual route-maps

WALK 1

10 miles

OVER FLASBY FELL

from Skipton

A lengthy march from the 'gateway to the Dales' to the colourful and shapely fells watching over it

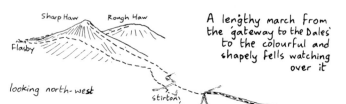

Sharp Haw   Rough Haw

Flasby

looking north-west

Stirton

by-pass

Skipton

Use one of the central car-parks in Skipton

NB : the walk can be substantially reduced by starting from the vicinity of Tarn House, Stirton

THE WALK

From the war memorial-roundabout at the top of the High Street, take the Grassington road past the church and the Castle Inn, and over a bridge. Turn immediately right along a lane (Chapel Hill) which climbs steeply to end at a gate and stile: thus we have made an exceptionally rapid escape from the town to the country. Climb straight up the field to a stile at the very top close by the site of the old battery. From here continue in the same direction towards the by-pass, which is gained by crossing a farm-lane parallel with it. Cross with care and from a stile on the other side head directly away again, to a stile which admits to Skipton golf-course.

Continue straight across, passing a short section of wall to arrive at the wall ahead, with a small length protruding our way. Take the stile on the left and follow the fence away, crossing one final stile before accompanying a left-hand fence down onto Brackenley Lane. Turn left up the lane to it's junction with the Skipton-Grassington road, and cross to a stile directly opposite. Aim for a stile at the far side of the field, then head away from it alongside a fence which soon falls into disrepair: continue up the gentle slope to reach a gate onto a lane just above Tarn House.

Turn right along the lane and at the third sharp bend reached, take a gate on the left to follow a wide, gently-rising track. After two more gates open country is entered: when the accompanying wall breaks off to the left, leave the track by bearing off to the right. On climbing the slope a faint path materialises, and improves as the top of Sharp Haw is neared and the going steepens a little. A stile in the wall across the top admits to the trig. point on Sharp Haw's airy summit. Neighbouring Rough Haw is across the depression to the north, and is our next objective. Follow the path along the short ridge for a few yards, then it drops to the right to a gateway in the wall there. The path heads straight down the slope and across the depression to a gate, from where the main path heads left. The short scramble onto Rough Haw is worthwhile though, and involves climbing the steep path directly ahead, to pass through an outcrop of rocks before levelling out to reach the cairn.

On returning to the gate, take that path heading away; it soon descends gradually through bracken, past a wood and across a tiny beck to a gate in the bottom corner. Continue along the edge of the field to another gate, from where an enclosed track winds down to the farmyard of Flasby Hall Farm. The rest of Flasby lies across the bridge over the beck, but our return route starts before the first barns on the left, along a wide track heading left.

This track runs by a wood then climbs left to a farm, running along the front of it. From the bridge beyond, it rises through a field to enter Crag Wood at a gate. A good path heads away from it, soon swinging up to the left to a footpath sign indicating a fork to the right. Take this path, which descends a little then heads left for a few sketchy yards to emerge through a gap onto the sharp bend of a wide forest road. Take the branch to the left, which heads away on a generally level course. Follow this track all the way to the point where it swings left to be seen to leave the trees for open country. Do not follow it to the gate however, but take a path forking to the right to leave the wood by a gate after a few yards.

Head across the field, over the beginnings of a beck to a stile beyond. Follow the wall away to a gate, then cross a fence and follow it away again to another gate, just beyond which a final gate leads onto a lane. Turn right for a short distance, then from a stile on the left head half-right across the field (two trees in the centre guide the way) to a kissing-gate onto another lane. Go right for just a short distance on a footpath alongside the lane, and at the end of the caravan park it branches left to a stile. From it head

Flasby

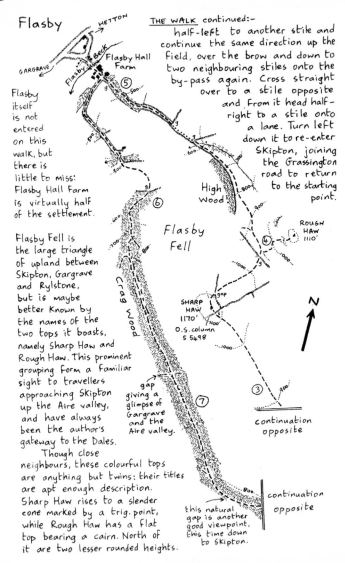

GARGRAVE

Flasby Beck

Flasby Hall Farm

⑤

500—

Flasby itself is not entered on this walk, but there is little to miss: Flasby Hall Farm is virtually half of the settlement.

Flasby Fell is the large triangle of upland between Skipton, Gargrave and Rylstone, but is maybe better known by the names of the two tops it boasts, namely Sharp Haw and Rough Haw. This prominent grouping form a familiar sight to travellers approaching Skipton up the Aire valley, and have always been the author's gateway to the Dales.

Though close neighbours, these colourful tops are anything but twins: their titles are apt enough description. Sharp Haw rises to a slender cone marked by a trig. point, while Rough Haw has a flat top bearing a cairn. North of it are two lesser rounded heights.

THE WALK continued:—

half-left to another stile and continue the same direction up the field, over the brow and down to two neighbouring stiles onto the by-pass again. Cross straight over to a stile opposite and from it head half-right to a stile onto a lane. Turn left down it to re-enter Skipton, joining the Grassington road to return to the starting point.

High Wood

ROUGH HAW 1110'

Flasby Fell

⑥

④

Crag Wood

SHARP HAW 1170' O.S. column S 5498

gap

⑦

gap giving a glimpse of Gargrave and the Aire valley.

③

continuation opposite

N

continuation opposite

this natural gap is another good viewpoint, this time down to Skipton.

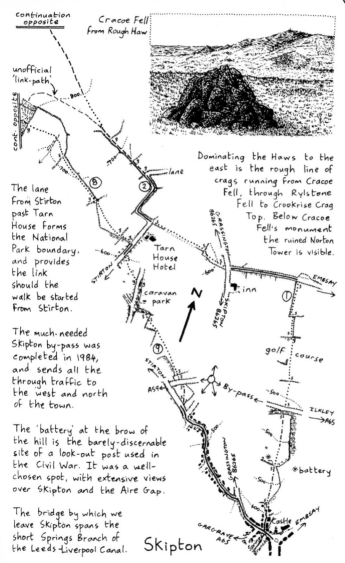

continuation
opposite

Cracoe Fell
from Rough Haw

unofficial
'link-path'

cont. opposite

800

700

700

⑧

⑨

②

lane

The lane
from Stirton
past Tarn
House forms
the National
Park boundary,
and provides
the link
should the
walk be started
from Stirton.

600

STIRTON

Tarn
House
Hotel

caravan
park

Dominating the Haws to the
east is the rough line of
crags running from Cracoe
Fell, through Rylstone
Fell to Crookrise Crag
Top. Below Cracoe
Fell's monument
the ruined Norton
Tower is visible.

GRASSINGTON B6265

600

inn

SKIPTON B6265

①

EMESAY

N

golf   course

The much-needed
Skipton by-pass was
completed in 1984,
and sends all the
through traffic to
the west and north
of the town.

STIRTON

A59

BY-PASS

500

ILKLEY
A65

500

The 'battery' at the brow of
the hill is the barely-discernable
site of a look-out post used in
the Civil War. It was a well-
chosen spot, with extensive views
over Skipton and the Aire Gap.

GRASSINGTON B6265

500

500

*battery

The bridge by which we
leave Skipton spans the
short Springs Branch of
the Leeds-Liverpool Canal.

500

GARGRAVE
A65

Castle

EMESAY

Skipton

15

WALK 2

MALHAM COVE AND BEYOND

5 miles

from Malham

A very easy walk through stunning limestone scenery A must!

looking north-east

Use the large car-park in the village

THE WALK

From the car-park pass through the village, keeping left at the junction by the bridge. After the cluster of buildings at Town Head the lane begins to climb: we soon leave it by a gate signposted on the right, with the majestic Cove already in full view directly ahead. A path leads to the very foot of the cliffs, but to go further, retrace steps a little to climb the man-made steps round the left side of the Cove. A stile at the top leads to the limestone pavement covering the Cove-top. Great care must be taken on crossing it, for the grikes in between have a great leg-damaging capability.

Having reached the centre of the Cove-top a wall is met: ignore both the stile and the gate however, and follow our side of the wall away from the Cove. After a stile in an intervening wall the crags on either side close in as we proceed along the floor of Watlowes, the Dry Valley. At the dramatic valley-head the path escapes by climbing to a stile in front, from where we swing sharp right alongside a fence to round a ledge under Dean Moor Hill. Soon the outcrops are left behind and a wall provides company across the open moor to lead unerringly to Water Sinks.

A line of telegraph-poles indicate the proximity of the road across the moor, and is soon reached at a gate by following the beck upstream. Turn right along the road as it starts to run freely across the moor, and soon a footpath sign indicates the Pennine Way crossing at right-angles to the road. Follow it's course to the right, and we now make use of the way to return to the Cove. Beyond a wall the extensive

Prior Rakes is crossed, then three more walls are encountered as we pass through the well-defined trench of Trougate between low outcrops. On meeting another path follow it back down to the right to return to the wall at the top of Malham Cove.

Re-cross the limestone pavement and return to the foot of the Cove. Use the path back to Malham as far as the first gate, and then cross the beck by means of a footbridge of stone slabs. Turn right up the slope, and a faint path rises towards the first of three stiles in cross-walls. Continue on to a gap in a collapsing wall, and then follow the wall to the right to reach a stile. After a few enclosed yards, head away in the same direction with a wall now on the left. On reaching a small shelter, the way becomes enclosed again, and remains so to re-enter Malham in fine style. Debouching onto a back-lane, continue straight down past the youth hostel into the village centre.

Malham Cove

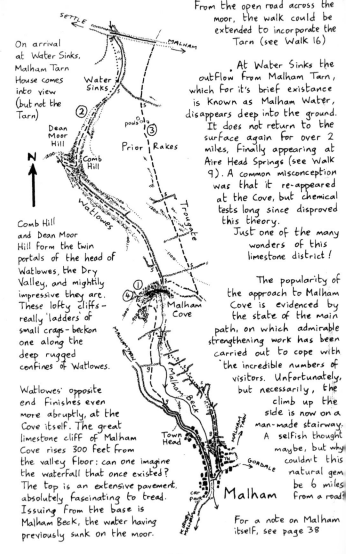

On arrival at Water Sinks, Malham Tarn House comes into view (but not the Tarn)

Comb Hill and Dean Moor Hill form the twin portals of the head of Watlowes, the Dry Valley, and mightily impressive they are. These lofty cliffs — really 'ladders' of small crags — beckon one along the deep rugged confines of Watlowes.

Watlowes' opposite end finishes even more abruptly, at the Cove itself. The great limestone cliff of Malham Cove rises 300 feet from the valley floor: can one imagine the waterfall that once existed? The top is an extensive pavement, absolutely fascinating to tread. Issuing from the base is Malham Beck, the water having previously sunk on the moor.

From the open road across the moor, the walk could be extended to incorporate the Tarn (see Walk 16)

At Water Sinks the outflow from Malham Tarn, which for it's brief existance is known as Malham Water, disappears deep into the ground. It does not return to the surface again for over 2 miles, finally appearing at Aire Head Springs (see Walk 9). A common misconception was that it re-appeared at the Cove, but chemical tests long since disproved this theory.

Just one of the many wonders of this limestone district!

The popularity of the approach to Malham Cove is evidenced by the state of the main path, on which admirable strengthening work has been carried out to cope with the incredible numbers of visitors. Unfortunately, but necessarily, the climb up the side is now on a man-made stairway. A selfish thought maybe, but why couldn't this natural gem be 6 miles from a road?

For a note on Malham itself, see page 38

WALK 3

6¼ miles

from Winterburn

An easy circuit of a lovely sheet of water,
returning via a splendid old house

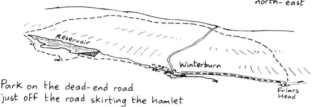

looking
north-east

Park on the dead-end road
just off the road skirting the hamlet

THE WALK

From the T-junction head up the dead-end
road through the heart of the hamlet: on reaching a cattle-
grid it becomes a private farm-road, crossing a length of
pasture by the beck to arrive at a bridge. Cross it and
follow the road along to the right, still alongside the beck.
After a while it gradually climbs above the beck to arrive
at the reservoir-keeper's house, with the top of the dam
being easily accessible through the gate in front. Our route
however does not quite reach the house, for we turn up
the farm-road branching left at a right-angle, before another
branch even nearer the house. Climb the farm-road which
leads circuitously but unerringly to Way Gill Farm.

Cross the cattle-grid into the confines of
the farm, then follow the fence on the right to a gate,
thereby leaving the farm almost immediately. Continue on to
a gate in the wall just ahead, then head half-right down
the field to a gate in the fence across the bottom. From
it the farm-road to High Cow House is joined, and by
following it to the left the farm is soon reached. Pass along
the front of the main building, through a gate and straight
on to another gate just ahead. In view now is the bridge at
the head of the reservoir, and a path slopes down towards it,
becoming enclosed as the bridge is neared.

Across the bridge is a large expanse of
rough pasture, and an indistinct path heads up it, half-
left for a few yards only and then turning right to rise

gradually. The path remains sketchy throughout, levelling out to arrive at a gate in a wall descending towards the right. The gate marks the end of a walled track, but once on it leave immediately by a gate on the right, to head over another rough pasture to a conspicuous gap in the line of trees ahead A path leads through the narrow plantation, then leaves us in an immense tract of rough pasture. Head directly away from the trees, aiming for a small cluster of trees which, on nearing, surround a farmhouse. As we converge with the wall across to the right, two barns are passed: stay outside the farm's confines and after a gate continue behind the farm itself to another gate.

A large dome-like pasture is entered, without a path or sign of exit. Panic not however, but aim diagonally away from the gate, and straight over the brow of the field using the graceful peak of Sharp Haw as an infallible guide. Passing a wall corner on the right, descend to the far corner and use a gateway a few yards to the right. From it follow the wall on the left, passing two barns and remaining with the same wall to emerge onto the Hetton—Winterburn road.

Cross to the gate immediately opposite and head straight down to a gate in the corner, then continuing by the wall to eventually reach another gate at the far end. Head away again with the wall now on the right, and from a gate in a fence bear right to drop to a gate in the corner. Now simply accompany the wall on the right down onto the lane, directly opposite Friars Head. Turn right along the lane for a short level walk back into Winterburn.

Winterburn is a small farming community set in an attractive location between the hills. Here is a former chapel of 1703, one of the first Independent chapels. It was restored early this century

Friars Head is a superb 17th century house, the most interesting in the district. Here was a grange of the monks of Furness Abbey, and farm-life still thrives.

An excellent viewpoint for a last look at the rugged skyline from Cracoe Fell to Flasby Fell

Winterburn Reservoir is a substantial finger-like sheet of water, and one could be forgiven for believing it, at first glance, to be natural. Even the dam with it's grass cover seems to blend in well. A clue to the reservoir's purpose is seen just prior to reaching the bridge at it's head: by the path a stone inscribed 'LLC' indicates that the reservoir was constructed to supply the Leeds–Liverpool Canal at Gargrave. Now, there is a strong air of neglect: the Keeper's house is boarded up and a variety of bird-life take advantage of this peaceful setting.

High Cow House Farm

Way Gill Farm

②

Farm road

700

Winterburn Reservoir

Moor Lane

N

①

Winterburn Beck

600

Long Hill Farm

③

The head of Moor Lane is something of a Piccadilly Circus of footpaths, for a guide-post points in no less than five directions, namely to, Bordley, Hetton, Threshfield, Winterburn and Malham. Don't go astray here!

The Winterburn valley is split into two very different sections by the reservoir: downstream is a deep, heavily-wooded confine, while the head of the reservoir points to extensive moor-like terrain.

700

④

Owslin Laithe

WINTERBURN

HETTON

600

NB: if time is pressing, this lane will cut off the last corner of the walk, but you'll forfeit this→

Friars Head

WALK 4

4¼ miles

KIRKBY MALHAM AND THE AIRE

from Airton

A gentle ramble
over rolling hills
and along the
riverbank

looking
north-west

Parking can
be found alongside
(but not encroaching) Airton's green,
or on the main road.

THE WALK

Leave Airton's green by the telephone-box
at the south-west corner, crossing straight over the main
road and up the lane opposite, signposted to Hellifield.
Shortly after the last buildings take a gate on the right, with
another one just behind it. Head away from it along the
field-edge to a gate at the far end, and then continue to
a gate by a barn to follow a short track out onto the
Settle-Airton road. Take this pleasant lane up to the left,
encountering a more level section before reaching two stiles
directly opposite each other.

Opt for the one on the right and climb by
the wall, passing a small plantation to a stile on it's left.
Continue down by the wall leading away, to a stile at the
bottom beyond which is a tiny beck. From it follow the
wall no longer, but instead bear across the field along a
conspicuous groove sloping left. At the fence at the far end
go left to a stile, crossing straight over a farm-track and
descending steeply alongside a fence: Kirkby Malham is now
at our feet. From the stile in the corner head half-right
to the next one, continuing the direction to a small gate to
enter the trees below. Steps descend to a footbridge spanning
Kirkby Beck, then up onto a lane by the church.

Turn right, over the crossroads by the inn and
down the lane opposite to Hanlith Bridge. Cross it to a
stile on the right and accompany the river downstream. The
Aire is clung to, through a gate then two neighbouring
stiles to arrive at a footbridge. Cross it and make for a stile

22

in the wall downstream, continuing on to the start of the old leat, which is also a footbridge. The path is now sandwiched between mill-leat and river, remaining like this to wind round to the converted mill. Pass round to the right of the mill, into the car-park and out onto a lane: Airton village green is just up to the right.

From Scosthrop Lane to entering Kirkby Malham, our walk follows an old way known as Kirk Gait. This, as it's name suggests, is the route taken by the good folk of Otterburn (see Walk 7) to reach the Parish Church at Kirkby Malham. A glimpse at an O.S. map will confirm the practical, direct way they chose.

For more on Kirkby Malham see Walk 9

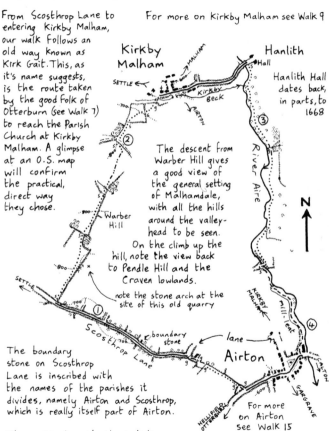

Kirkby Malham

SETTLE ←

Hanlith

Hanlith Hall dates back, in parts, to 1668

River Aire

N

The descent from Warber Hill gives a good view of the general setting of Malhamdale, with all the hills around the valley-head to be seen.

On the climb up the hill, note the view back to Pendle Hill and the Craven lowlands.

note the stone arch at the site of this old quarry

Warber Hill

SETTLE ←

Scosthrop Lane

boundary stone

lane →

Airton

For more on Airton see Walk 15

MELLBERR OTTERBURN

GARGRAVE

mill-leat

AIRTON

The boundary stone on Scosthrop Lane is inscribed with the names of the parishes it divides, namely Airton and Scosthrop, which is really itself part of Airton.

The walk alongside the leat to Airton Mill is an interesting mini-history trail. The imposing mill, which once spun cotton, is well-preserved as individual flats.

WALK 5

8½ miles

CROOKRISE CRAG TOP

From Embsay

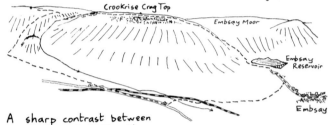

looking north-east

Crookrise Crag Top

Embsay Moor

Embsay Reservoir

Embsay

A sharp contrast between moorland and field-paths. The scenery on the outward leg is simply superb

Use the car-park at the top end of the village, just past the Elm Tree Inn

THE WALK

From the car-park return to Elm Tree Square and leave the main road by continuing along Pasture Road, which after passing a mill and it's old pond climbs to the dam of Embsay Reservoir. On approaching the reservoir it becomes a rough track, passing along the edge of the water (not across the dam). At the end it's confining walls break away and a stile gives access to the open moor. From it keep left on a path which meets another from the farm across to the left before accompanying the wall uphill. Staying near the wall the path further improves and passes through some characterful bouldery scenery before levelling out. Soon a stile in the wall is reached: use it to attain the top of the cliffs of Crookrise, a breathtaking moment. Now confined in the narrow space between the steep drop and the wall, continue northward, straight towards the white trig. point which soon comes into sight. At 1361 feet, this is Crookrise Crag Top.

After surveying the extensive panorama, take the stile there to return to the moorland side of the wall, and once again continue northward. On reaching Hellifield Crags (the second and much more substantial rock outcrops met) the steep drop to Waterfall Gill is encountered. The worst of this is avoided as a sketchy path slopes across to the right, past the lower boulders of Hellifield Crags to meet the beck without having lost too much height. Just before reaching the beck a fine waterfall should be seen from up above: don't miss it. Once across, accompany the crumbling wall as it climbs the bank, the gradient soon eases and the wall eventually leads to a gateway where the Rylstone – Bolton Abbey track passes through. Our route takes advantage of this way, and we turn through the gateway to follow it down the fell. After two gates a small plantation is reached: here the right-of-way forks left of the trees, leaving the main track. Both however join the same enclosed track at the foot of the pasture.

Turn left along this pleasant by-way and on reaching a gate continue alongside the remaining wall, doing similar when the wall switches to our right at the next gate. At the far end a walled track is again joined but after another gate it swings right to approach Sandy Beck Bar along a modest avenue of trees. From the gate there the track passes the large house to join the Skipton to Grassington road. A short mile of road-walking in the Skipton direction is unfortunately the low-spot of this walk as this tends to be one of the busier of 'B'-class roads. The first building we meet is None-Go-Bye Farm, and with sighs of relief turn down the track just past it.

This track heads down the field away from the farm, and after crossing the beck fork right through a gate to a grouping of barns. Without entering their yard, pass in front to a stile in the wall corner. From here slope up to the railway line, following it to an intervening stile before a stile leads us across the line itself. From a stile on the other side turn right to a gate, then on through a gateway in a collapsed wall to arrive at Hagg Farm via another gate. Pass between the buildings and out into the field beyond, to locate a stile in the far top corner.

Our way is now straightforward, for although pathless we simply accompany the wall on the left through numerous pastures with stiles or gates in between, but always remaining on the same contour. On reaching Oddacres Farm the buildings are avoided by a gate in the wall to the right. Continuing on, the cluster of farm buildings at Hill Top are next encountered. A stile by a blocked gate leads into the yard: go straight on to a gate ahead, then drop to a footbridge which leads back onto the lane to Embsay Reservoir. A right-turn takes us back into the village.

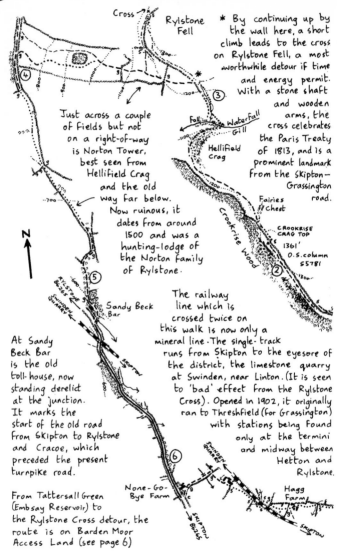

Cross → Rylstone Fell

Rylstone Fell

* By continuing up by the wall here, a short climb leads to the cross on Rylstone Fell, a most worthwhile detour if time and energy permit. With a stone shaft and wooden arms, the cross celebrates the Paris Treaty of 1813, and is a prominent landmark from the Skipton-Grassington road.

Fall ← Waterfall Gill

Hellifield Crag

Fairies chest

Crookrise Wood

CROOKRISE CRAG TOP 1361' O.S. column SS781

Just across a couple of Fields but not on a right-of-way is Norton Tower, best seen from Hellifield Crag and the old way far below. Now ruinous, it dates from around 1500 and was a hunting-lodge of the Norton family of Rylstone.

N

RYLSTONE SUNDEN?

Sandy Beck Bar

The railway line which is crossed twice on this walk is now only a mineral line. The single-track runs from Skipton to the eyesore of the district, the limestone quarry at Swinden, near Linton. (It is seen to 'bad' effect from the Rylstone Cross). Opened in 1902, it originally ran to Threshfield (for Grassington) with stations being found only at the termini and midway between Hetton and Rylstone.

At Sandy Beck Bar is the old toll-house, now standing derelict at the junction. It marks the start of the old road from Skipton to Rylstone and Cracoe, which preceded the present turnpike road.

SKIPTON

None-Go-Bye Farm

SKIPTON ROAD

Hagg Farm

SKIPTON

From Tattersall Green (Embsay Reservoir) to the Rylstone Cross detour, the route is on Barden Moor Access Land (see page 6)

left to climb gently to Nappa Gate, passing an old shaft on the way. The gate marks the high point of the walk.

After the gate leave the path and turn right on a lesser one, passing Nappa Cross and sloping across to a gate. Two further gates are encountered as the path makes it's way down the fell, soon reaching a gate in a corner, and then descending a pasture to meet the lane out of the village at Langscar Gate. Cross straight over to another gate and head down the field: when a stile appears in front, turn sharp right to reach a prominent stile in the wall there. The path, though sketchy, is reasonably easy to follow as it runs roughly parallel with the road up to the right.

After crossing an intervening collapsed wall, two further ones are crossed by stiles, from where an improved path leads to two more in very quick succession. Malham Cove is now just across to the left, but our way continues, sketchily again, to two more neighbouring stiles, the latter returning us onto the lane. Turn uphill for a short distance to a sharp bend, and here take a gate on the left: a track heads down to a gate where it becomes enclosed by walls to lead in pleasant fashion back past an earlier junction and down to a T-junction. To include the village at the finish, turn left here and almost immediately right to land in the village opposite Beck Hall. A right turn will lead back to the car-park.

above: the cairn on Pikedaw,
      looking to Kirkby Fell

left: Nappa Cross,
     looking to Malham Tarn

Nappa Cross is one of several way-side crosses in the area, a guide-post for travellers since monastic times. Set into the wall, the restored shaft stands in it's original base.

All three of the ways encountered on this west side of Malham are historic routes bound for the Settle district

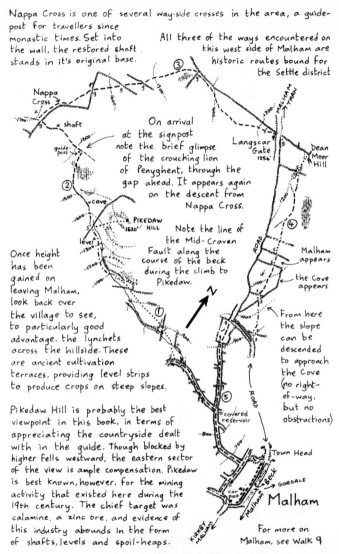

On arrival at the signpost note the brief glimpse of the crouching lion of Penyghent, through the gap ahead. It appears again on the descent from Nappa Cross.

Note the line of the Mid-Craven Fault along the course of the beck during the climb to Pikedaw.

Once height has been gained on leaving Malham, look back over the village to see, to particularly good advantage, the lynchets across the hillside. These are ancient cultivation terraces, providing level strips to produce crops on steep slopes.

From here the slope can be descended to approach the Cove (no right-of-way, but no obstructions)

Pikedaw Hill is probably the best viewpoint in this book, in terms of appreciating the countryside dealt with in the guide. Though blocked by higher fells westward, the eastern sector of the view is ample compensation. Pikedaw is best known, however, for the mining activity that existed here during the 19th century. The chief target was calamine, a zinc ore, and evidence of this industry abounds in the form of shafts, levels and spoil-heaps.

For more on Malham, see Walk 9

WALK 7

5½ miles

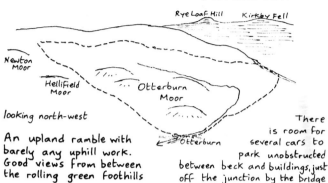

OTTERBURN MOOR

from Otterburn

Rye Loaf Hill   Kirkby Fell

Newton Moor

Hellifield Moor   Otterburn Moor

looking north-west

Otterburn

An upland ramble with barely any uphill work. Good views from between the rolling green foothills

There is room for several cars to park unobstructed between beck and buildings, just off the junction by the bridge

THE WALK

Leave the junction by the bridge along the unsignposted lane between Otterburn Beck and farm buildings. Almost immediately it becomes a wide track, and beyond a gate it runs free alongside the beck. On approaching another gate, leave the track by a gate on the right, and from it head half-left across the field to pick up a track rising towards a line of trees. From there head across to the top side of the wood in front, then accompany it's upper boundary to a gate. Head straight across the field to a stile in the far corner, ignoring a neighbouring stile in the right-hand wall. Follow this wall away in the same direction as before, and when it parts company continue over the brow of the field: pick out a stile in the wall ahead, bearing left towards it to emerge onto Scosthrop Lane.

Turn left up this pleasant lane only as far as a walled farm-road striking off to the left. Head along it's undulating course, which leads unerringly to Orms Gill Green, passing around the back of the farm buildings and continuing up the slope beyond. At the second cattle-grid after the farm the track becomes completely unenclosed, and after this grid leave it by heading half-left across the extensive open pasture. Aim for the bottom of the band of trees that appear ahead: as we near them Otterburn Beck appears down to the left, and where these two features meet, a stile will be found in the very corner. From it the beck is crossed

31

to an isolated signpost at a crossroads of footpaths: opt for the one climbing the slope behind. At the top it peters out, but continue on a sheep-trod past a wall-corner and then slope down to a stile in the wall ahead. This is one of the two walls enclosing the green road of Langber Lane.

Turn left along this wide by-way, all the way to it's unfortunate demise when the right-hand wall parts company. Cross the stile and remain faithful to the left-hand wall, taking in another stile in a fence before arriving at a gate by a wall-junction. On the other side a track is picked up leading from the small building on the left, and it takes us down through the pasture to a gate. Here it disappears, but resumes it's journey from the gate at the bottom of this field. Now entering a plantation the track continues without problem through the trees, emerging as a wide enclosed track known as Dacre Lane to descend very gently into Otterburn. On reaching the road turn left to round a corner to return to the junction by the bridge.

The bridge, Otterburn

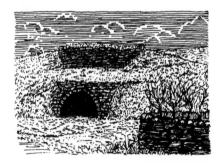

The old kiln Orms Gill Green

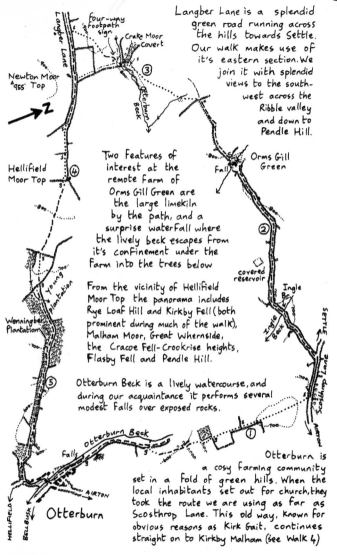

Langber Lane is a splendid green road running across the hills towards Settle. Our walk makes use of it's eastern section. We join it with splendid views to the south-west across the Ribble valley and down to Pendle Hill.

four-way footpath sign

Crake Moor Covert

③

Otterburn Beck

Newton Moor 'q55' Top

Langber Lane

Hellifield Moor Top

④

Orms Gill Green

Fall

②

covered reservoir

Ingle Br.

Ingle Beck

SETTLE

Scosthrop Lane

Two features of interest at the remote farm of Orms Gill Green are the large limekiln by the path, and a surprise waterfall where the lively beck escapes from it's confinement under the farm into the trees below

From the vicinity of Hellifield Moor Top the panorama includes Rye Loaf Hill and Kirkby Fell (both prominent during much of the walk), Malham Moor, Great Whernside, the Cracoe Fell–Crookrise heights, Flasby Fell and Pendle Hill.

Young Plantation

Wenningber Plantation

⑤

Otterburn Beck is a lively watercourse, and during our acquaintance it performs several modest falls over exposed rocks.

①

AIRTON

Otterburn Beck

Falls

HELLIFIELD

BELL BUSK

AIRTON

Otterburn

Otterburn is a cosy farming community set in a fold of green hills. When the local inhabitants set out for church, they took the route we are using as far as Scosthrop Lane. This old way, known for obvious reasons as Kirk Gait, continues straight on to Kirkby Malham (see Walk 4)

WALK 8

3½ miles

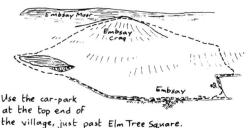

looking north

A lively circuit, taking in a grand hill with a surprise view

Use the car-park at the top end of the village, just past Elm Tree Square.

THE WALK

Leave the car-park not by it's entrance, but by a stile opposite it, and climb up the field half-right to another stile. An enclosed path leads away to a stile from where a large field is crossed, bearing a little left to emerge onto a lane via a small gate. Turn to the left up this lane, past the church to a sharp bend, and 50 yards beyond, leave it by a farm-road rising up between the houses. It rises to the farm-entrance, whereupon we go straight forward to a stile, to maintain the uphill plod to a gate. Above it the path peters out, but continue up to a gate at the top-left corner to gain access to the open moor.

Take the path along to the left, which soon leaves the wall to rise towards the striking profile of Embsay Crag. As the ground steepens the path keeps above the increasing tumble of rocks to rise pleasantly to the highest point of the Crag, a location which is not in doubt. The main path can clearly be seen descending the steepest section directly below, and is well-blazed through the bracken beyond. A much nicer way down, however, is to follow a very sketchy path along the brink of the rocks across to the right: this descends in similar fashion to our route of ascent, and after exchanging the heather for bracken another path is met. Turn left along it to join up with the main path down from the Crag. This path leads unerringly down to a footbridge by the head of the reservoir, having earlier passed a left fork which takes in the old quarry (see map).

34

From the footbridge avoid boggy ground by bearing half-right to join a wide track, which followed to the left leads to a stile ushering us from the open moor. Turn left along the farm-track down the side of the reservoir and onto a lane which leads all the way down into Embsay, emerging into Elm Tree Square.

Embsay Crag is a notable landmark in the Skipton area of upper Airedale, jutting out as it does from the vast expanse of moorland. A rich cloak of bracken covers the lower slopes, while a delectable carpet of heather crowns the top. The 'Crag' is actually a tumble of modest crags and large boulders heaped together in wonderful chaos on the southern slopes of the hill.

This is gritstone country at it's best, and the highest rocks are a perfect location for a long, lazy break on a hot summer's day, with the reservoir shimmering far below our airy vantage point.

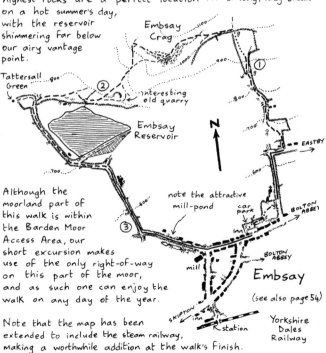

Although the moorland part of this walk is within the Barden Moor Access Area, our short excursion makes use of the only right-of-way on this part of the moor, and as such one can enjoy the walk on any day of the year.

Note that the map has been extended to include the steam railway, making a worthwhile addition at the walk's finish.

35

WALK 9

3¾ miles

from Kirkby Malham

A perfect combination of upland views and valley features

Park near the crossroads by the inn, there being some space across the bridge. The inn has it's own car park also.

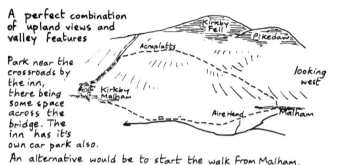

An alternative would be to start the walk from Malham.

THE WALK

From the crossroads by the bridge head up the back lane past the inn and church and round to a T-junction. Turn up the lane to the left, gaining height rapidly and passing a farm-road to New Close before reaching the track forking right to Acraplatts. Follow it over a cattle-grid, and just past it take a stile on the right. Descend the field to another stile, then pass a ruined barn to a tiny footbridge over Tranlands Beck. From it head across the field without losing height, to be deflected left by a wall to a stile by another tiny beck. From it slope up gently across the field to another stile, then follow a wall on the right to drop down through two more stiles and through a larger field to a gate. Behind it is an enclosed track which leads all the way down into Malham village, emerging next to the car-park.

Turn left towards the village, but as the road meets the beck take a stile into a field on the right. With a wall separating us, follow the beck downstream, crossing a stile, then Tranlands Beck (again), and another stile. As the beck swings away to the left, continue straight ahead to arrive at the emerging waters of Aire Head Springs. From the stile just beyond continue alongside a wall: the next stile returns us nearer the river, by now having merged with the beck. An improving path now leads above a former mill-pond, whose leat leads to the former mill. Pass round the top side of it to it's entrance gate. Instead of following the drive away, take the grass rake sloping to the right up to a stile, then head half-right to another and

36

straight on to the next one. This stile is just next to the lane as it enters Kirkby Malham, and it takes us into a field to walk parallel with the lane to join it at a gate. Turn left along the lane to return to the village centre.

Aire Head Springs is the point of re-emergence of the beck that last saw the light of day at Water Sinks high on the moor (see Walk 2). It is not therefore the source of the Aire but it *is* certainly the first naming of the River Aire. Almost immediately after it's resurgence (which after heavy rain becomes one mighty spring) the water joins with the newly-merged Malham and Gordale Becks to flow in unison as the Aire.

Malham

YH GORDALE

in car park

KIRKBY MALHAM

Malham Beck

From the vicinity of Acraplatts the prospect of the rugged Pikedaw is particularly impressive.

Good view to the Cove

②

'In memory of William Wilkinson of Keighley, who loved the Dales'

Acraplatts (farm)

Aire Head Springs

memorial seat

③

N

The extensive mill-pond below Aire Head remains in good condition, as does the leat which we follow to the former manorial mill. This is now well-maintained as a dwelling.

old mill

River Aire

This track gives an alternative return into Kirkby Malham via Hanlith Bridge

SETTLE

milestone

900

MALHAM

Easily missed, this old milestone is inscribed thus: 'To Settle 5 miles'

800

700

Hanlith

Kirkby Malham

AIRTON

Once height is gained on the climb out of Kirkby Malham, the view across to the vale of Malham provides an excellent insight into the topography of the area, with Kirkby Fell and Weets Top guarding each side of the valley, and Malham, the Cove and the heights of the Moor in between.

Kirkby Malham is, ecclesiastically at least, the main village of Malhamdale, although most visitors to the valley drive through almost without notice on their way to the tourist mecca of Malham. This tiny village is however worth a brief exploration, and not surprisingly the parish church is of most interest. Dedicated to St. Michael the Archangel, this highly attractive building dates from the 15th century and was restored a century ago, thanks mainly to Walter Morrison of Malham Tarn House: his memorial can be seen in the church. Also of note are a Norman font and a 16th century German window. Oliver Cromwell is reputed to have signed the register as witnessing a marriage during his stay in the district in the Civil War.

In the churchyard is an ancient preaching cross, and near the lych-gate are the former village stocks. The church is sandwiched by two other buildings of note, namely the inn at the bridge-end and the Old Hall just up the lane. Running alongside is Kirkby Beck, which joins the Aire a good quarter-mile from the village.

Monk Bridge, Malham

Malham is an attractive village whose appeal is very different to that of most other Dales villages, in that the *majority* of it's visitors come to walk, even though for most it's simply a return trip to the Cove. The village itself does however have much of interest, both old and new. A good number of cottages date from the 17th and early 18th centuries, and form several attractive groups.

In monastic times the land hereabouts was shared between Bolton Priory and Fountains Abbey, and reminders of their granges here are found in the naming of two of the numerous bridges over Malham Beck which divides the village in two. Monk Bridge was once a packhorse bridge, now widened to form the road bridge, while Prior Moon's Bridge is the highest of the several clapper-bridges. Both the inns are centrally placed along with two modern purpose-built structures, namely the youth hostel and the National Park Information Centre.

WALK 10 | BORDLEY AND THRESHFIELD MOOR | From Boss Moor

7½ miles

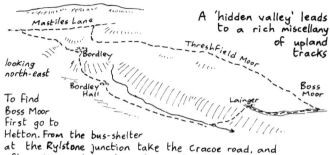

A 'hidden valley' leads to a rich miscellany of upland tracks

looking north-east

To find Boss Moor first go to Hetton. From the bus-shelter at the Rylstone junction take the Cracoe road, and after 100 yards a lane forks left, signposted 'Bordley 4'. Half-way up it emerges onto the open moor, and almost at once an obvious parking place is seen on the right, with a guide-post and an old quarry in close proximity.

THE WALK

Before even starting, take a glance over the wall for a most complete view of Winterburn Reservoir, with Pendle Hill directly behind. The walk commences with a gentle stroll along the lane towards Bordley, as far as the phone box and farm at Lainger. Here leave the lane by the farm-track down to the left, accompanying a beck to cross the main beck in the valley bottom. Take a stile on the right to follow Bordley Beck upstream, over another stile and then across to a gate to the left of a small group of trees. From it a good path heads across the bracken high above the beck, but fades away as soon as the bracken does. Our way is deflected left by a tributary beck, which is crossed to another gate. Follow the wall away from it, through a gateway and across a bridge over a small beck to arrive at Bordley Hall.

Enter the farm's confines, following the track between the buildings and out at the far end. Without crossing the watersplash, turn sharp left on a lesser track, leaving it to climb the path-less field to a gate. In the large field behind, a gate appears in the top wall. With the gradient easing, head half-right to locate a hidden stile in the corner. From it a farm-track is joined to head through two gates to Bordley. Turn left in the hamlet on the track to the top corner, and a good track heads away from the gate. In a few yards take a lesser track right, rising gently and becoming less clear before it joins Mastiles Lane at a crumbling gateway. Follow it to the right: beyond a gate it's less-clear course hugs the left wall to become enclosed again at Mastiles Gate. Here we sadly leave the lane by turning right on a faint track through a hollow, to arrive at a crossroads of ways marked by a guidepost. Turn left, through a gateway and up the tarmac arm.

As this lane levels out, branch across to the right to peer over the wall at the stone circle. The wall can then be followed left to rejoin the lane as it becomes enclosed. This quiet way is now trod for a long half-mile, to the point where guideposts indicate a junction with a bridle-path. From the gate on the right a string of posts guide us along a sketchy level track. At another gate we descend more clearly past a barn and along an enclosed way to a gate at the far end. From it a track heads right, crossing a small beck to head across the open moor, again with marker-posts assisting. On reaching a wall, a pleasant walled green track leads to the next section of moor but here we remain with the right-hand wall as far as a gate. This leads onto Boss Moor, positively the last lap.

across ↗

Bordley Hall

← continued

A good track heads diagonally away from the gate, and with the Bordley lane soon in view, our track avoids it until reaching the old quarries and all being well, the car.

→ Z

Threshfield Moor

Boss Moor

old quarries

Threshfield Moor provides extensive views, notably of Great Whernside (north) and the Cracoe and Flasby fells (south).

Bordley is a tiny farming hamlet standing at a breezy 1100 feet above sea-level. It's remoteness is stressed by the fact that several lanes head towards it, but none actually reach it as public roads.

The solid stone buildings are spread around a large green, which is workmanlike rather than picturesque. The hamlet is sheltered from the worst of the weather by virtue of it's position in a hollow in the hills.

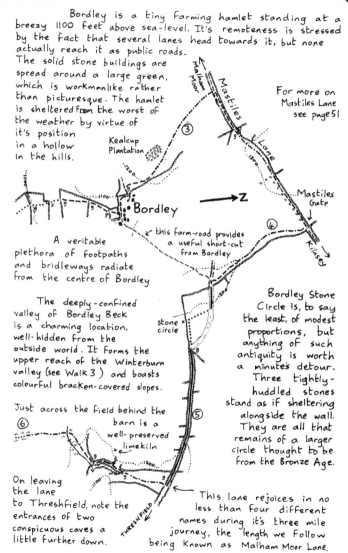

Kealcup Plantation

③

Malham Moor

Mastiles Lane

For more on Mastiles Lane see page 51

Bordley

→ Z

Mastiles Gate

④

Kilnsey

← this farm-road provides a useful short-cut from Bordley

A veritable plethora of footpaths and bridleways radiate from the centre of Bordley

The deeply-confined valley of Bordley Beck is a charming location, well-hidden from the outside world. It forms the upper reach of the Winterburn valley (see Walk 3) and boasts colourful bracken-covered slopes.

stone circle

Bordley Stone Circle is, to say the least, of modest proportions, but anything of such antiquity is worth a minutes detour. Three tightly-huddled stones stand as if sheltering alongside the wall. They are all that remains of a larger circle thought to be from the Bronze Age.

Just across the field behind the barn is a well-preserved limekiln

⑥

⑤

On leaving the lane to Threshfield, note the entrances of two conspicuous caves a little further down.

THRESHFIELD

This lane rejoices in no less than four different names during it's three mile journey, the length we follow being known as Malham Moor Lane.

WALK 11

5¾ miles

from Gargrave

looking
north-west

Haw Crag

Eshton

R. Aire
Gargrave

A rural stroll,
calling for
little effort

Gargrave has
ample free
car-parking

THE WALK

Leave the main street in Gargrave along West Street, almost opposite the bridge over the Aire, and at the second car-park continue straight ahead over the canal bridge. Ignore any turn-offs and remain on this leafy by-way for a gradual uphill march: shortly after the demise of the trees on the right, take a stile into the field on the same side. Remain parallel with the lane for a short distance, then strike across the field, past a solitary tree to a stile. In the next field take the first opportunity to rise to a stile on the left, continuing the climb to the corner of the plantation on Harrows Hill.

A gate in the fence ahead is ignored in favour of a stile a little further to the left, from where one strikes diagonally across the field to another stile. Maintain this course to accompany the field boundary to a gate in the far corner. From it head off diagonally again to arrive at the sharp angle of a fence. For a while now, the white Ordnance column on Haw Crag has been in sight, and as a right-of-way runs through it's field a 10-minute detour is worth the effort On returning to the fence follow it's right arm down to a gate, from where a farm-track heads down to become enclosed by fences to arrive at Throstle Nest Farm.

Head straight on between barns, leaving on a track which swings right, avoiding the maze-like confines of the farm by continuing on to a stile when the track re-enters the farmyard. From the stile the farm access-road is joined, and is accompanied out onto a lane. Turn right to descend to the junction at Eshton, keeping right until after passing by Eshton Grange a stile is seen on the right. Take it and make for a stile in the fence ahead, then cross the field to another stile. Across the next narrow field a kissing-gate leads into the woods, and a good path heads through trees, passing a large remote dwelling before emerging from near-claustrophobic conditions into a large field. Descend straight down to an iron stile and maintain the same course to a stile to emerge onto the road just past a junction.

Double back to this junction and then turn right as far as the bridge over the canal. Here leave the road to join the towpath, following it along to the right and forsaking it at the next but one bridge encountered. This completes the full circle of the walk, and a left turn along the lane will return us to the car-parks on West Street.

Gargrave is an attractive village and is the best centre for the Craven Dales. Although Skipton is the main centre for the southern Dales, and is only 10 minutes distant by road, Gargrave has a far more

The War Memorial and Main Street, Gargrave

intimate Dales atmosphere. The village is split by the busy A65 running through it, and the by-now sizeable Aire runs parallel. Lined by shops, the main street widens into a spacious area by the war memorial, and here a graceful bridge crosses the river to get to the Parish Church. Dedicated to Saint Andrew, it was restored in 1852 : the tower, however, dates from the early 16th century.

The Pennine Way passes through the heart of the village, and the two central inns provide appropriately-placed lunchtime breaks for those midway between the youth hostels at Earby and Malham. The Leeds — Liverpool Canal also comes this way, reaching the northernmost point of its 127 miles as it meets, if only briefly, the National Park boundary. The waterway takes advantage of the Aire Gap to squeeze its way through the Pennines. Our mighty backbone also gives its name to the homespun bus firm based in the village, and their orange livery may well be seen threading the lanes hereabouts.

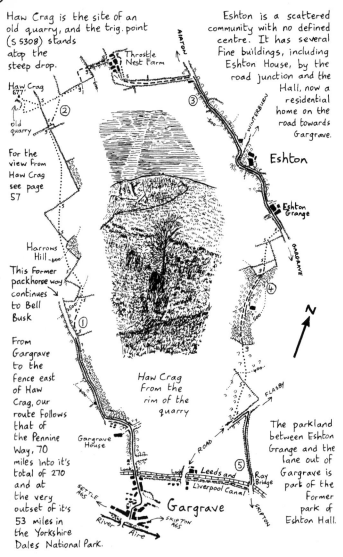

Haw Crag is the site of an old quarry, and the trig. point (S 5308) stands atop the steep drop.

Haw Crag 677

old quarry

② 5

For the view from Haw Crag see page 57

AIRTON

Throstle Nest Farm

Eshton is a scattered community with no defined centre. It has several fine buildings, including Eshton House, by the road junction and the Hall, now a residential home on the road towards Gargrave.

③ 500

WINTERBURN

Eshton

Eshton Grange

GARGRAVE

④ 600

Harrows Hill 600

This former packhorse way continues to Bell Busk

① 5

From Gargrave to the fence east of Haw Crag, our route follows that of the Pennine Way, 70 miles into its total of 270 and at the very outset of its 53 miles in the Yorkshire Dales National Park.

Haw Crag from the rim of the quarry

FLASBY

N

Gargrave House

ROAD

The parkland between Eshton Grange and the lane out of Gargrave is part of the former park of Eshton Hall.

Lock Leeds and Liverpool Canal ⑤ Ray Bridge

SETTLE A65

SKIPTON

Gargrave

River Aire

SKIPTON A65

44

WALK 12

4¾ miles

From Flasby

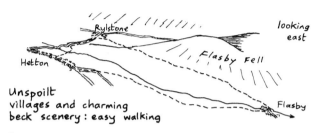

looking
east

Rylstone

Hetton

Flasby Fell

Flasby

Unspoilt
villages and charming
beck scenery: easy walking

Park in one of the few roadside locations in the hamlet

THE WALK

      Flasby stands just off the Gargrave - Hetton
road, and a choice of two lanes wind down to it. Head
down the dead-end road over the bridge and into the yard
of Flasby Hall Farm. Take the track on the left after the
last building, and follow it through a gate and around the
edge of a field: at the other side keep going to a gate
near the far corner. Head away from it alongside a fence
on the left, and at the next gate a better track returns
to lead straight to the farm of Flasby Moor Side.
      Cross the farmyard to the diagonally-opposite
corner, and after passing the last building turn right to climb
the field to the plantation at the top. A path leads through
the narrow strip of trees, and from the other side head away
to descend a large field to the initially unseen Calton Gill Beck.
From a stile and a footbridge head up the next field to the
conspicuous bridge under the railway line. From the other side
head half-left to locate a stile at the end of the plantation
in front. Head across the bottom of the next field, and at the
gate at the far end a track is joined: follow it left at the
next gate and then right at a T-junction of enclosed tracks.
At the farm buildings at the end, turn left along a lane
which curves round to join the road on the edge of Rylstone,
which is just up to the right and well worth a look.
      Our way turns left, under the railway bridge
and then along the track immediately to the left. It soon
narrows into a delightful snicket, descending to a footbridge

45

(a stone slab) over the beck, and then rising between hedges to debouch onto the road through Hetton: the inn is but a few yards to the right. Once again however, our route turns left, and stays left as the road forks: within a minute a stile on the left is reached. Aim half-left across the field to a stile in the wall ahead, and do likewise in the next field, this stile being just above the beck. The beck is followed to the next stile, from where our sketchy path is deflected away by trees: do not return to the beck, but continue across to a stile in the wall ahead, with another shortly after.

Beyond this is a stile in a fence from where a broad 'ridge' descends parallel with the beck to arrive at another stile. Continue across the next field to a stile nearer the beck, beyond which the farm-road to Flasby Moor Side is crossed. From the stile just across it, take a gate almost immediately on the left, but instead of rejoining the beck follow the fence up the slope. When it breaks off to the right continue straight ahead, and a conspicuous mound is followed high above the beck to descend gradually to a barn. Just past it, take a gate almost next to the beck, which is now followed to the next gate. From it bear right across two small enclosures to emerge through a gate back onto the lane in Flasby.

Rylstone is the tiniest of villages, but there is much of interest here. Alongside the main road is the attractive pond, fringed in April by daffodils, and once the village green. Near the church was the home of the Norton family, who took part in 1536 in the

Pilgrimage of Grace, and three years later the Rising of the North. Their unfortunate story is recounted by Wordsworth in his 'White Doe of Rylstone'.

The parish church of St. Peter stays prominent even though it hides up a back lane. Rebuilt in 1852, it's position is an envious one, gazing across to Rylstone Fell with it's cross clearly visible. Look also for the medieval gravestones with crosses.

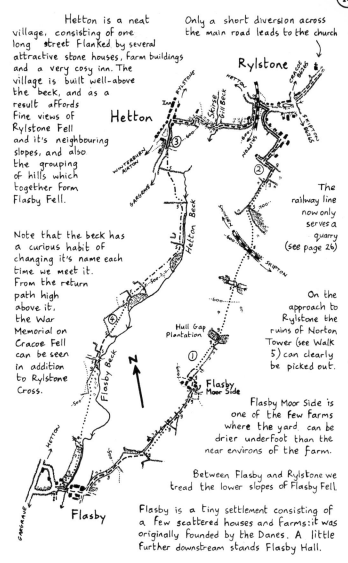

Hetton is a neat village, consisting of one long street flanked by several attractive stone houses, farm buildings and a very cosy inn. The village is built well-above the beck, and as a result affords fine views of Rylstone Fell and it's neighbouring slopes, and also the grouping of hills which together form Flasby Fell.

Only a short diversion across the main road leads to the church

Note that the beck has a curious habit of changing it's name each time we meet it. From the return path high above it, the War Memorial on Cracoe Fell can be seen in addition to Rylstone Cross.

The railway line now only serves a quarry (see page 26)

On the approach to Rylstone the ruins of Norton Tower (see Walk 5) can clearly be picked out.

Flasby Moor Side is one of the few farms where the yard can be drier underfoot than the near environs of the farm.

Between Flasby and Rylstone we tread the lower slopes of Flasby Fell.

Flasby is a tiny settlement consisting of a few scattered houses and farms: it was originally founded by the Danes. A little further downstream stands Flasby Hall.

WALK 13

9½ miles

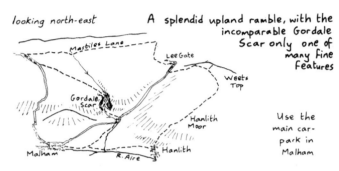

| GORDALE, MASTILES LANE AND WEETS TOP |

from Malham

looking north-east

A splendid upland ramble, with the incomparable Gordale Scar only one of many fine features

Use the main car-park in Malham

THE WALK

From the car-park head into the village, crossing the beck by the road-bridge and doubling back to follow the beck downstream. The short lane ends at a stile, from where a good path heads across the fields. After two more stiles the path swings left to a barn, crosses to the left of the wall and continues in the same direction. One stile later Gordale Beck is joined and followed all the way upstream to enter the wooded environs of Janet's Foss. On reaching the waterfall the path breaks off left to emerge onto the road to Gordale. Turn right along it for a short distance, crossing the beck and arriving at a gate on the left just before Gordale House. A well-trod path heads across the pasture to the unmistakeable cliffs of Gordale Scar, which converge on us as we enter the dark confines.

The way out is by negotiating the rock to the left of the lower falls: it is a straightforward short scramble with plentiful hand-holds, but nevertheless care is necessary (please don't fall on anyone). Having clambered up, the stony path clings to the left side of the gorge, passing the upper falls and breaking out onto green pastures once more. Beyond a stile the path becomes sketchy, but this matters little for the way appears fairly obvious as it passes through low outcrops. A long low line of the said outcrops deflect our path to the left, and a long trek ensues before arriving at a stile onto the moor-road to Malham Tarn. Follow this right, keeping by the wall when the road swings away, to arrive at a gate with an old sign pointing the way towards Grassington. This is Street Gate, and it signals the commencement of our march along Mastiles Lane. The walking is easy and pleasant as the track clings to the right-hand wall, even though in places it is not always clear on the ground. At a gate the way becomes confined, and shortly before the next gate in the lane we leave it by a gate on the right, where a good track doubles back alongside a fence.

This track becomes fully enclosed to drop down past the isolated Lee Gate Farm, with whose access road we merge to join the head of Smearbottoms Lane. Head along this undulating strip of tarmac to leave it by the second walled track on the left, which rises immediately to arrive at Weets Cross. Through the gate adjacent to it will be found, just up to the left, the Ordnance column marking Weets Top. Returning to the gate, a good path heads away from it beginning a gentle descent of the moor. Soon a guide-post on the right indicates a stile in the wall there, and from it a path heads across Hanlith Moor with a succession of marker-posts serving to confirm the route. Eventually a gate is reached, through which the rough track of Windy Pike Lane leads our steps unfailingly down into Hanlith.

Do not drop down all the way to the river, but at the second sharp bend in Hanlith (a left-hander) go straight on to the right, through the gate on the right of a farm. Contour across the field to be channelled into a stile alongside a gate, and continue along the top of a wood. In the next field a vague path contours the indentation of a tiny beck before descending another field to a footbridge over Gordale Beck. From the fence behind it head well to the left of the barn ahead, and at the economy-size stile our outward leg is rejoined. Retrace those first few steps back into the village, with a small stone clapper bridge providing an equally-small short-cut back to the car-park.

Weets Cross

From Hanlith back to Malham we follow the Pennine Way. On several occasions in the Malham area the popularity of that walk is emphasised by the provision of two adjacent stiles, but near Malham Beck we find ingenuity in the shape of a double-width stile.

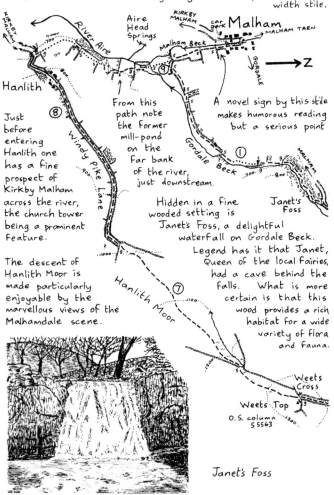

Kirkby Malham · River Aire · Aire Head Springs · KIRKBY MALHAM · CAR PARK · Malham · MALHAM TARN · Malham Beck · ⑨ · GORDALE · → Z · Malham

Hanlith

Just before entering Hanlith one has a fine prospect of Kirkby Malham across the river, the church tower being a prominent feature.

The descent of Hanlith Moor is made particularly enjoyable by the marvellous views of the Malhamdale scene.

Windy Pike Lane

From this path note the former mill-pond on the far bank of the river, just downstream.

A novel sign by this stile makes humorous reading but a serious point

Gordale Beck · ① · MALHAM

Janet's Foss

Hidden in a fine wooded setting is Janet's Foss, a delightful waterfall on Gordale Beck. Legend has it that Janet, Queen of the local Fairies, had a cave behind the falls. What is more certain is that this wood provides a rich habitat for a wide variety of flora and fauna.

Hanlith Moor · ⑦

Weets Cross

Weets Top

O.S. column SS563

Janet's Foss

It should be noted that at Gordale Scar one needs to partake of a short climb on rock — this is a fairly simple task with ample hand-holds, but may nevertheless be outside the scope of certain less-agile walkers. It is beyond all non-amphibious walkers after a good deal of rain. The best alternative is to return to Gordale Bridge from where a marked path crosses to the Malham Tarn road, for Street Gate, or straight across to return to Malham via the Cove.

✻ This walk is particularly suitable for breaking down into two separate shorter rambles, by using the traffic-free Smearbottoms Lane (becoming Hawthorns Lane) as a link back to and out of Malham, for the two walks respectively.

MALHAM TARN

MALHAM

Street Gate

Z

Gordale Bridge

Gordale Beck

Gordale House

Gordale Scar

Mastiles Lane is probably the most famous of old roads in the district. This classic green lane was used by the Monks of Fountains Abbey to cross from Kilnsey to their valuable sheep-rearing pastures in the Malham area. Look out for the base of a wayside cross (see map). The Lane is at it's most inspiring when fully enclosed by walls. Note the large boulders incorporated into the lane's north wall - they are boundary stones separating Malham and Bordley.

cross base

Mastiles Lane

GORDALE

Smearbottoms Lane

Kilnsey

Weets Top is one of the finest viewpoints in the area, with most of the features in the southern Dales in sight. Quite a number of parish boundaries meet here, and the restored Cross serves to mark this point.

Lee Gate

Gordale Scar is probably the most awe-inspiring single feature of the Yorkshire Dales. Unlike the Cove at Malham, which bears all on first sighting it, the Scar has a far more intriguing nature, waiting for the visitor to turn the final corner before impressing him to the full.

Once in it's dark confines the grandeur of the overhanging cliffs up above can initially be a little too daunting to fully appreciate the waterfalls: the upper fall spills in spectacular fashion through a circular hole in the rocks. The water is that of Gordale Beck, being funnelled from the lonely moors to the green valley.

above: the waterfalls

Gordale Scar

below: the approach

52

WALK 14

7 miles

EMBSAY MOOR

from Embsay

looking north

Embsay Moor

Embsay Crag

Embsay   Eastby

A classic moorland ramble

Use the car-park at the top end of the village, just past Elm Tree Square

THE WALK

From the car-park return to Elm Tree Square and continue straight along the back lane (Pasture Road), which leaves the village on passing a mill, and rises to the foot of the dam of Embsay Reservoir. Follow the track up left, past the dam top and along the side of the reservoir. When the wall is replaced by a fence, take a stile in it to gain access to the open moor. Accompany the track away for only yards until crossing a tiny stream, then look for a vague path branching left. Though not easy to locate initially, an upper section can be more clearly seen, rising across the moor at a steady angle. Once joined this becomes an easy-to-follow shooting-track. The gradient soon eases and a most enjoyable trek across the moor ensues. After reaching the brow of East Harts Hill, a gradual descent is made to cross the upper reach of Waterfall Gill, from where the track climbs sharply to arrive at two attractive shooting-houses.

Just above these buildings the track merges into the Rylstone-Bolton Abbey bridle-track, which is sketchy to the west, but a pleasant wide track as we accompany it eastward thanks to it's modern use as a shooting-track. This way is trod for about two miles, and it is generally level throughout. A branch to Embsay is ignored long before we leave the track, our point of departure being where a footpath sign indicates a crossroads. An inviting green path heads off left, but ours is the pathless way to the right, aiming straight for two modern shooting-houses. Here a good track is met and followed up between the two buildings. With a row of grouse-butts appearing to the left, the track soon peters out: head across and follow their line away. From the last one bear a little left to a stile which takes us off the moor.

A sketchy path bears right to descend the fields to a gate, another stile, and then drops down more directly and well-defined through several more stiles. The way becomes more confined in it's lower section to emerge onto the lane in Eastby. Turn right, leaving the village and then leaving the road at a stile on the left. A clear path now heads diagonally across the fields, aiming directly for the church. On reaching the road, follow it for only a few yards down past the church, then opt for a small gate on the right. Aim half-left across the field to a stile, from where an enclosed path leads to another stile. Just below is Embsay's car-park, and a final stile leads back into it.

Embsay Moor

cairn and stake

grouse butts

④

1300

excellent view of Lower Barden Reservoir from here onwards

The two shooting-huts above Waterfall Gill come as quite a surprise, being traditionally constructed of local stone with a delightful thatch-like topping. Even the shape is rather unique.

③

1300

shooting huts

Waterfall Gill

One of the greatest joys of walking is crossing heather moors on good paths, and in this vicinity we are indeed well-favoured. Note the crudely-paved section on this highest point.

East Harts Hill

1300

grouse butts

②

grouse butts

1300

N

1100

Partly inside the National Park boundary, Embsay is a thriving and sizeable village, perfectly sandwiched between Skipton town and the open moors. It was here the Augustinians began work before opting for the Wharfe's banks to found Bolton Priory. Today Embsay is the home of a preserved railway, and a most enjoyable hour or two can be spent on a good honest steam train.

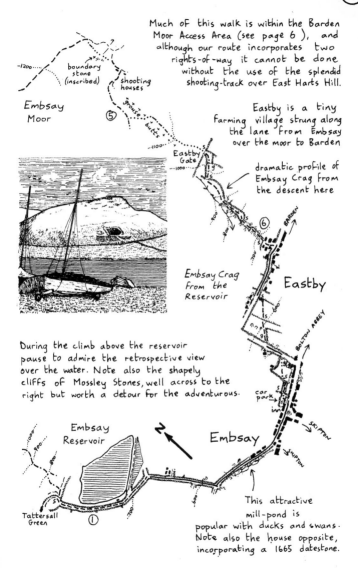

Much of this walk is within the Barden Moor Access Area (see page 6), and although our route incorporates two rights-of-way it cannot be done without the use of the splendid shooting-track over East Harts Hill.

Embsay Moor

boundary stone (inscribed)

shooting houses

⑤

grouse butts

Eastby Gate

Eastby is a tiny farming village strung along the lane from Embsay over the moor to Barden

dramatic profile of Embsay Crag from the descent here

⑥

BARDEN

Eastby

BOLTON ABBEY

Embsay Crag from the Reservoir

During the climb above the reservoir pause to admire the retrospective view over the water. Note also the shapely cliffs of Mossley Stones, well across to the right but worth a detour for the adventurous.

car park

inn

SKIPTON

Embsay Reservoir

Embsay

SKIPTON

Tattersall Green

①

This attractive mill-pond is popular with ducks and swans. Note also the house opposite, incorporating a 1665 datestone.

55

WALK 15

5 miles

from Airton .

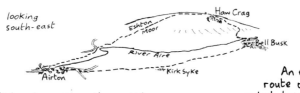

looking
south-east

Airton has reasonable roadside
parking, notably by the green
(but definitely NOT on it)

An easy
route over
modest heights
and along a
lovely riverbank

THE WALK

Leave the green by the telephone-box at the
south-west corner, crossing straight over the main road and
up the lane opposite (signposted Hellifield). Turn off it at the
first opportunity along a lane to the left. This lane is also
soon forsaken, this time along an enclosed track to the right.
This farm-track is followed throughout it's entire length, past
the farm at Kirk Syke and then past a grouping of barns. A
little past a gate, the track becomes sketchy as it's left-hand
boundary disappears. The way remains clear however, passing
an old quarry, two ponds and a barn to emerge into a field.
Head straight on with a fence on the right to a gate ahead,
with the fence switching to the left to reach the next gate. A
large field is entered: follow the fence down to the barn, in
front, behind which is a bridge over Otterburn Beck. From it
a clear track leads past some barns onto the lane in Bell Busk.

Turn left along this lane, leaving it upon
reaching a road-bridge over the beek. On crossing, fork right
immediately along a lesser lane to cross a bridge over the Aire.
It then heads uphill: on levelling out we pass an isolated
dwelling, and the way becomes rougher, turning sharp left to
climb again. Leave it at the next sharp bend right, taking the
gate directly ahead to enter the pasture containing Haw Crag.
Head straight up the slope to the edge of the old quarry, and
then follow the rim around to the Ordnance column marking
the highest point.

On leaving, re-trace steps along the rim and
then swing left to rejoin the original line, arriving at a
prominent gate in the wall ahead, with a less prominent stile

alongside it. Again head directly across the field to arrive at an acute angle in a fence: here the Pennine Way is joined and now followed all the way back to Airton. Accompany the left branch of the fence down to two stiles in the corner of the field, then follow the wall away as far as a gate in it. Do not use the gate, but instead bear gradually away from the wall to avoid a large dog-leg in it, descending the large field till walls converge alongside a road. This narrow, enclosed way takes us down to a stile on the left, and a small beck leads us left to a footbridge over the River Aire.

From the bridge follow the riverbank upstream, entering the wood on the left by a stile when there is no more room on the bank. Another stile leads back out of the trees, and the river again leads us upstream towards Newfield Bridge, a stile to it's left emptying onto the road there. Cross the bridge and take a stile on the left to rejoin the river once more. From a stile by a gate follow the wall straight ahead, nearing the river again at two stiles in quick succession. From the second leave the river again for a stile in the next wall along, and then head across the large pasture, closing in on the river as Airton Bridge comes into view. From the stile to it's right, cross the bridge to climb the lane back onto the green at Airton.

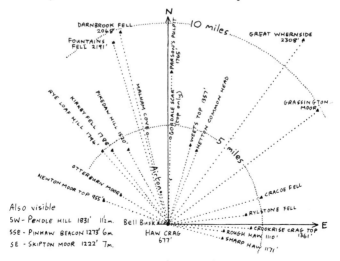

The principle features of Craven from Haw Crag

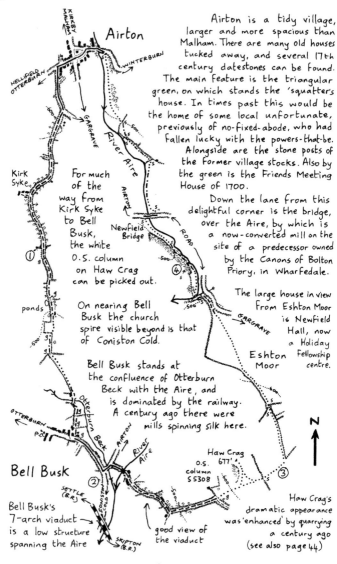

Airton is a tidy village, larger and more spacious than Malham. There are many old houses tucked away, and several 17th century datestones can be found. The main feature is the triangular green, on which stands the 'squatter's house. In times past this would be the home of some local unfortunate, previously of no-fixed-abode, who had fallen lucky with the powers-that-be. Alongside are the stone posts of the former village stocks. Also by the green is the Friends Meeting House of 1700.

Down the lane from this delightful corner is the bridge, over the Aire, by which is a now-converted mill on the site of a predecessor owned by the Canons of Bolton Priory, in Wharfedale.

The large house in view from Eshton Moor is Newfield Hall, now a Holiday Fellowship centre.

KIRKBY MALHAM

Airton

WINTERBURN

HELLIFIELD OTTERBURN

GARGRAVE

River Aire

Kirk Syke

For much of the way from Kirk Syke to Bell Busk, the white O.S. column on Haw Crag can be picked out.

AIRTON

Newfield Bridge

ROAD

GARGRAVE

Eshton Moor

ponds

On nearing Bell Busk the church spire visible beyond is that of Coniston Cold.

Bell Busk stands at the confluence of Otterburn Beck with the Aire, and is dominated by the railway. A century ago there were mills spinning silk here.

OTTERBURN

Otterburn Beck

AIRTON

River Aire

P°

N

Bell Busk

Haw Crag O.S. column SS308

Haw Crag 677'

SETTLE (B.R.)

CONISTON COLD

SKIPTON (B.R.)

Bell Busk's 7-arch viaduct is a low structure spanning the Aire

good view of the viaduct

Haw Crag's dramatic appearance was 'enhanced' by quarrying a century ago (see also page 44)

WALK 16   ┌─────────────────────────┐
                        │ AROUND MALHAM MOOR │
                        └─────────────────────────┘
8 miles   From Malham Tarn

A bracing ramble combining limestone uplands
with the environs of Malham Tarn

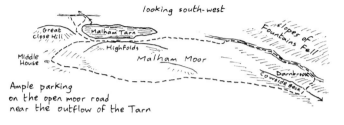

looking south-west

Ample parking
on the open moor road
near the outflow of the Tarn

THE WALK

From the gate where the road crosses the beck
follow the unenclosed road east for a couple of minutes,
as far as the guide-post indicating the crossing of our old
friend the Pennine Way. Turn left along the Way, on a
green track which heads directly to a gate to merge with
the main track to the Malham Tarn estate. Follow this track
along the shore of the tarn until arriving at a cattle-grid
at the entrance to a wood: do not enter, but instead climb
the slope to the right. A green track materialises to swing
right as the gradient eases, nearing a fence but not
crossing it. As the fence bends left on the hill-top, the
track soon fades: simply follow the fence down to a stile.
From there follow the fence leading away to the isolated
Middle House Farm, and on reaching another stile don't cross
it but turn left to climb the field to a gate.

From this gate a good track heads across
the limestone pasture, but within a minute or so take a
fork right to join a wall there. Passing a cluster of
barns embowered in trees, the path crosses a collapsed
wall to a guide-post: here we leave the Arncliffe path
and take the rather sketchier left fork. It contours round
a hollow below some small outcrops to arrive at a stile,
and beyond the wall heads away through more outcrops
to fade completely as the ground slopes away. Follow the
line of rocks downhill, with the farm at Darnbrook appearing
ahead. As the wall below appears, look for a cairn just
across to the right: it marks a fine viewpoint worth the

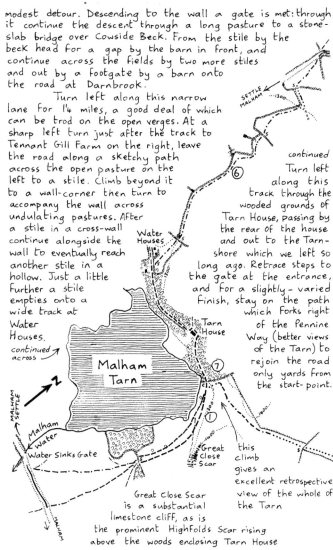

modest detour. Descending to the wall a gate is met: through it continue the descent through a long pasture to a stone-slab bridge over Cowside Beck. From the stile by the beck head for a gap by the barn in front, and continue across the fields by two more stiles and out by a footgate by a barn onto the road at Darnbrook.

Turn left along this narrow lane for 1¼ miles, a good deal of which can be trod on the open verges. At a sharp left turn just after the track to Tennant Gill Farm on the right, leave the road along a sketchy path across the open pasture on the left to a stile. Climb beyond it to a wall-corner then turn to accompany the wall across undulating pastures. After a stile in a cross-wall continue alongside the wall to eventually reach another stile in a hollow. Just a little further a stile empties onto a wide track at Water Houses.

continued across →

SETTLE ←
MALHAM ···1300.

continued

Turn left along this track through the wooded grounds of Tarn House, passing by the rear of the house and out to the Tarn-shore which we left so long ago. Retrace steps to the gate at the entrance, and for a slightly-varied finish, stay on the path which forks right of the Pennine Way (better views of the Tarn) to rejoin the road only yards from the start-point.

Water Houses

Tarn House

Malham Tarn

↗ N

MALHAM
SETTLE

Malham Water
Water Sinks Gate

Great Close Scar

this climb gives an excellent retrospective view of the whole of the Tarn

Great Close Scar is a substantial limestone cliff, as is the prominent Highfolds Scar rising above the woods enclosing Tarn House

This partially unfenced road provides an exhilarating drive over the tops to Littondale. Sadly (?) those gates so frustrating to the passengerless driver are now replaced by cattle-grids.

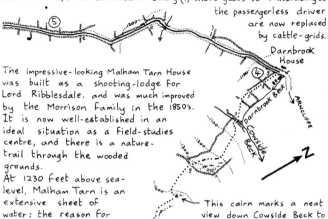

Darnbrook House

The impressive-looking Malham Tarn House was built as a shooting-lodge for Lord Ribblesdale, and was much improved by the Morrison family in the 1850's. It is now well-established in an ideal situation as a field-studies centre, and there is a nature-trail through the wooded grounds.

At 1230 feet above sea-level, Malham Tarn is an extensive sheet of water: the reason for it's existance in this limestone preserve is a layer of Silurian slate on which it stands. This snippet of geological knowledge is one of the few survivors from many people's (including the author's) schooldays.

This cairn marks a neat view down Cowside Beck to the floor of Littondale, backed by the two tiers of Old Cote Moor and behind that, Buckden Pike.

Still evident here is the site of an ancient British settlement

guide post

The monks of Fountains Abbey held fishing rights on Malham Tarn, which is now home to a variety of birdlife. It was here that Charles Kingsley drew inspiration to create 'The Water Babies'. The estate is now in the safe hands of the National Trust.

Middle House

Winter on Great Close Scar, from the path to Malham Tarn

LOG OF THE WALKS

These two pages provide an opportunity to maintain a permanent record of the walks completed

WALK	DATE	TIME Start	Finish	WEATHER	COMMENTS
1					
2					
3					
4					
5					
6					
7					
8					

WALK	DATE	TIME Start	Finish	WEATHER	COMMENTS			
9								
10								
11								
12								
13								
14								
15								
16								

KEY TO THE MAP SYMBOLS

direction of north

scale
2½ inches = 1 mile

Route — clear — sketchy — no visible path

Route on public road — wall — unenclosed — fence/hedge

River/beck — bridge

Marsh

Peat grough

Crags

Limestone clints

Loose rocks/scree

Cairns
summit   other

Trees

Buildings

Church

Abbreviations
c = cattle grid
s = stile
g = gate

Miles from start
③

contours
(at intervals of 100 feet)
700
800

THE COUNTRY CODE

Respect the life and work of the countryside
Protect wildlife, plants and trees
Keep to public paths across farmland
Safeguard water supplies
Go carefully on country roads
Keep dogs under control
Guard against all risks of fire
Fasten all gates
Leave no litter - take it with you
Make no unnecessary noise
Leave livestock, crops and machinery alone
Use gates and stiles to cross fences, hedges
and walls